A VIEW FROM THE MARGINS

Stories for Holy Week

Sean Gladding

For Rev. Dr. John Smith,

(1942-2019)

who lived his life at the margins,

and encouraged so many of us to join him there.

Rest in peace, 'Bullfrog,'

and rise in glory.

And for his wife, Glena.

Whenever I see the word "margins"

I hear it with your accent.

Table of Contents

Preface

Every year during Holy Week, we are invited to step back almost 2,000 years in time. We join the huge crowds flooding into Jerusalem for Passover and watch as events unfold that will come to define our faith. Events that will make the cross the central symbol of Christianity, a symbol that, in time, would come to dominate the landscapes of Europe. And – sharing Constantine's vision, *in hoc signo vinces,* "in this sign, conquer" – a symbol that would come to dominate the landscapes of other continents. A symbol raised in all those lands that the Christian nations of Europe believed had need of the religion they had to offer, and from which those nations then plundered the resources those lands had to offer, regardless of whether they were actually offered to the colonizers or not.

When your religion dominates the landscape, it's easy to forget that it began, not at the center of empire in the seats of power, but at its margins. It's easy to forget that a symbol from which you draw comfort and strength originated as a tool of repression, and at times in history has been a symbol of oppression to those who suffered at the hands of those who carried the cross on shields and banners.

When you drive past any number of churches to get to the church to which you belong; when your money says, "In God We Trust"; when many of the public meetings you attend begin with a prayer

1

that ends, "In Jesus' name we pray," then it's easy to draw a straight line between the "triumphal entry" of Palm Sunday and the "triumph over the grave" of Easter Sunday. But in doing so we run the risk of missing what Jesus was doing during the days in between.

As we walk the narrow streets of Jerusalem this Holy Week we may naturally feel ourselves to be close to the action, already knowing what we're going to find thanks to the privileged view provided by centuries of Christianity. But perhaps this year we will hear the invitation to move from the center of the action to the margins, from where we might catch a very different perspective.

Then let us wrestle with the questions raised by a view from the margins.

Welcome to Holy Week.

A Note to the Reader

This collection of short meditations has its origins in a series of sermons I preached in Lexington, Kentucky for the Transylvania Presbytery during Holy Week in 2018. Several people asked me if I would make them available afterwards, which planted the seed which has grown into this short book.

I have taken some creative license in the way I tell these peoples' stories, filling out the details of their lives from my imagination. But I believe I have not strayed far from the truth of their situations, and I hope you will lean in with me to catch a view of Jesus from each character's place at the margins. Not every story will resonate. Some may irritate. Pay attention to the emotions each story provokes and ponder why those feelings may have arisen in you.

Each day's reading begins with a passage from the Gospels, followed by the story of one of the characters in the passage. It concludes with an invitation to engage in a form of the Examen, a daily practice of Ignatian Spirituality. There are many ways to engage in the Examen. I have adapted one version to offer this 6-step process for reflection:

1. Take a few moments to sit quietly and recognize God's presence with you.

2. As you think back over the reading, what are you most grateful for about what you read?

3. What feelings – comfortable and/or uncomfortable – arose as you read?

4. Choose one part of the story that particularly struck you and ask God what you're being invited to pay attention to.

5. Is there an invitation to take action of some kind? If so, make note of it, with the intention to follow through.

6. Rest in God's presence for a few moments.

I encourage you to carve out time each day to read the story and to practice the Examen. I have included space for you to write down what you hear during both the reading and the Examen. But even if you only have time to read the story, I hope you're able to engage your imagination and fully enter the experience of each protagonist. Whatever time is available to you, may you carry the stories with you throughout the week – and beyond – as we walk deeper into the darkness that precedes the light of Easter.

The action is by the disciples

Palm Sunday

After He had said these things, He was going on ahead, going up to Jerusalem. When He approached Bethphage and Bethany, near the mount that is called Olivet, He sent two of the disciples, saying, "Go into the village ahead of you; there, as you enter, you will find a colt tied on which no one yet has ever sat; untie it and bring it here. If anyone asks you, 'Why are you untying it?' you shall say, 'The Lord has need of it.'" So those who were sent went away and found it just as He had told them. As they were untying the colt, its owners said to them, "Why are you untying the colt?" They said, "The Lord has need of it." They brought it to Jesus, and they threw their coats on the colt and put Jesus on it. As He was going, they were spreading their coats on the road. As soon as He was approaching, near the descent of the Mount of Olives, the whole crowd of the disciples began to praise God joyfully with a loud voice for all the miracles which they had seen, shouting:

"Blessed is the King who comes in the name of the Lord; Peace in heaven and glory in the highest!"

Some of the Pharisees in the crowd said to Him, "Teacher, rebuke Your disciples." But Jesus answered, "I tell you, if these become silent, the stones will cry out!"

When He approached Jerusalem, He saw the city and wept over it, saying, "If you had known in this day, even you, the things which make for peace! But now they have been hidden from your eyes. For the days will come upon you when your enemies will throw up a barricade against you, and surround you and hem you in on every side, and they will level you to the ground and your children within you, and they will not leave in you one stone upon another, because you did not recognize the time of your visitation."

Luke 19.28-44

Imagine for a moment that you're a little boy growing up on the outskirts of a tiny village in the shadow of first century Jerusalem. The rhythm of your life is simple. At dawn you feed the animals, after which you walk to the synagogue in nearby Bethany with two of your siblings, where a scribe teaches you Torah – the Law of your people – mostly through memorization. You return home for a quick bite of flatbread dipped in olive oil, made from the handful of trees growing in front of your one room house. Then you take your family's small flock out to the hills to graze, returning at dusk for a meal. Finally, you crawl into bed.

Each day is much like the last, except for the sabbath of course. But a few times a year there are the Holy Days, with special meals and music and dancing! You especially look forward to Passover, when great crowds pass your village, singing the psalms of ascent on their way up to Jerusalem. And Passover is this week, although you can't join your father and your older brothers who will soon join the pilgrims traveling to Jerusalem for the Festival. Not until you come of age – something you very much look forward to!

While you're enjoying the midday meal of roasted grain and dried figs, you watch as two strangers approach the village. They pause, look around and when their gaze settles on your house, they immediately stride towards you. You call out nervously to your father, who is inside. The strangers smile at you, and then begin to untie your colt from the wooden rail! Your father walks out, sees them and says, "Why are you untying the colt?" One of the strangers says, "The Lord has need of it." Your father holds their gaze for a long moment, then nods. The men walk off with your colt, much to your amazement. You turn to your father, who says, "Go with them, and bring the colt back when the Lord is finished with it." You hesitate, but he shoos you off, and so you follow the men, confusion writ large on your face.

The men bring the colt to a group of people standing just off the main road up to Jerusalem. Some of the group shrug off their outer garments and place them over the back of the colt. As they assist a man onto the colt's back, you wait for the animal to buck, as no one has ever ridden it before. But it stands there meekly as the man settles himself. One of the men who came to get the colt takes its halter and leads it onto the road to join the crowd of pilgrims.

As you follow behind, you tug the robe of the other man and gesture towards the colt. "Who is that?" He smiles. "It's the Lord. Jesus of

Nazareth." You turn back to look at Jesus. Your parents have spoken of him, usually with a smile on their face. Not like the scribe in the synagogue, who spits on the ground whenever anyone says Jesus' name. *So that's who all the fuss is about*, you think to yourself. He's not much to look at, that's for sure. What's so special about him? But as the crowd around him notice the colt and its rider, they begin to part before him. Some take off their garments and throw them onto the road before him. How strange! Then they fall in behind the colt and raise their voices in joyful song.

As they begin to draw close to Jerusalem, someone begins to sing aloud,

> "Blessed is the King who comes in the name of the LORD;
> peace in heaven and glory in the highest!"

The crowd begins to join in, and soon everyone is singing the refrain over and over again. There is a joyful spirit about them, and everyone is smiling. Well, not everyone you realize, as you glance at some men wearing the distinctive garb of the pharisees. One calls out to Jesus.

> "Rabbi, rebuke your disciples!"

Jesus turns to the man and responds,

"I tell you, if they become silent, the stones by the roadside will cry out!"

The pharisees scowl, then scurry on ahead of the crowd as the people make their way leisurely into the city, continuing to sing the psalm. As you lift your voice in song with everyone else, one of the pharisees cuffs you on the ear as he passes. Tears of pain and shock stream from your eyes. Later that evening, as you walk home with the colt, you wonder what the pharisees were so upset about...

+ + +

Perhaps you're reading this before you join your church in worship this Palm Sunday. If so, it's quite possible you'll hear a sermon about Jesus's 'triumphal entry' into Jerusalem. Perhaps you'll sing one of the rousing hymns we often sing today – "Hosanna, loud Hosanna," or, "All glory, laud and honor." There may well be a parade down the center aisle involving children – and a few reluctant adults – waving palm branches. Palm Sunday often brings with it a festive atmosphere, and rightly so.

In Luke's Gospel we've been waiting for this moment for ten chapters, from verse 9.51, where Luke declares that "Jesus resolutely set his face to go to Jerusalem." And now, here is Jesus, about to enter the great city, the site of the Temple, which even now is preparing for the arrival of the pilgrim crowds which will swell the city's population to overflowing. Jerusalem was a tinderbox at

Passover. The people gathered to celebrate their ancestors' deliverance from the tyranny of pharaoh, to re-live the events of the exodus, all under the watchful gaze of the Roman soldiers drafted in to 'keep the peace.' You can almost taste the resentment in the air, but resentment blended with hope, the hope that God will finally act to deliver you from your enemies. Would *this* be the year when Messiah came to the Temple? Would this be the year when the long-awaited king of the line of David would overthrow the tyranny of your oppressors?

That appears to be what the crowds on the road up to Jerusalem believed was happening. Matthew, in his telling of the story, makes the case explicitly, by quoting the prophet Zechariah:

> "Behold your king is coming, gentle and mounted on a donkey, even on a colt."

And *that* is what appears to have infuriated the pharisees, who tell Jesus to silence his followers. Certainly, *they* don't believe that Jesus is the long-awaited Messiah. And it's one thing for these peasants to make claims about Jesus in the villages of Galilee: it is another thing entirely for them to do so in Jerusalem. It's one thing for them to speak against the Romans in their homes in the hills: it's another thing entirely to do so in the shadow of the Eagle standards raised in Jerusalem. No, "tell your people to be quiet, Jesus." This kind of behavior is unacceptable.
And dangerous.

+ + +

One of the primary ways people are marginalized is by denying them their voice. By telling them to be quiet.

To know their place.

And so, whenever the marginalized and oppressed dare to raise their voices in protest of their lived experience, in hope of change, there are always those who want them to be quiet. People who – like the pharisees – instruct the leaders among the oppressed to find another way for them to express their protest, one that is more acceptable. One that doesn't inconvenience others who may not share their views. One that respects the tight parameters permitted for protest.

Or better yet, for them to just go home and wait patiently for change to come.

Well, the people on the road to Jerusalem that day had waited for change to come for centuries. They had suffered under the boot of one empire after another, as well as at the hands of their own leadership, who often collaborated with the might of empire to maintain their own, privileged, position. So, when they saw the rabbi from Galilee who talked of a new Kingdom that was coming, who taught them with stories rooted in their own experience of life, a rabbi who stood in solidarity with them – the poor, the diseased, the outcasts, the despised – how could they keep quiet as they accompanied him to the city where they would celebrate God's deliverance of their oppressed ancestors? But even if they were to stop singing, Jesus responds to the critique of the pharisees:

"If these do become silent, I tell you the stones will cry out!"

+ + +

As we begin Holy Week, the invitation before us is to move to the margins, to see Jesus from a different perspective, as well as to look around us from that de-centered place. Most of us picture ourselves in that crowd, waving palm branches, throwing our jackets into the road ahead of Jesus, celebrating the King who rides on the back of that young boy's colt. Personally, I'm *always* up for the parade down the center aisle on Palm Sunday.

But am I also up for joining the crowds protesting systemic injustice today? To stand in solidarity with those who speak out against their plight? Especially when those crowds engage in behavior with which I may not be comfortable? As the Rev. Dr. Martin Luther King Jr. observed in a speech he gave just three weeks before he was assassinated,

"A riot is the language of the unheard."

The authorities in Jerusalem always feared riots during Passover. They knew any unrest would bring down the wrath of Rome upon their heads, as well as threaten the stability of the societal order, which – after all – worked very well for them. "No," say those with power, "if people feel they are treated unjustly there are appropriate channels for them to go through to express their concerns." Channels often created by – and overseen by – the very people with whom those suffering injustice have concerns.

Dr. King was jailed in 1963 following a non-violent protest against segregation in Birmingham, Alabama. Eight white clergymen made a public statement against him, describing the protest as "unwise, untimely and extreme." Dr. King wrote the now famous 'Letter from Birmingham Jail' in response, in which he decries those who are "more devoted to order than to justice; who prefer a negative peace which is the absence of tension to a positive peace which is the presence of justice."

"Teacher, tell your disciples to be quiet."

"I tell you, if they become silent, the stones by the roadside will cry out!"

+ + +

The Examen

1. Take a few moments to sit quietly and recognize God's presence with you.

2. As you think back over the reading, what are you most grateful for about what you read?

3. What feelings – comfortable and/or uncomfortable – arose as you read?

4. Choose one part of the story that particularly struck you and ask God what you're being invited to pay attention to.

5. Is there an invitation to take action of some kind? If so, make note of it, with the intention to follow through.

6. Rest in God's presence for a few moments.

Space for reflection – what did you hear?

SEAN GLADDING

Monday

Then they came to Jerusalem. And He entered the temple and began to drive out those who were buying and selling in the temple, and overturned the tables of the money changers and the seats of those who were selling doves; and He would not permit anyone to carry goods through the temple. And He began to teach and say to them, "Is it not written, 'My house shall be called a house of prayer for all the nations'? But you have made it a robbers' den." The chief priests and the scribes heard this, and began seeking how to destroy Him; for they were afraid of Him, for the whole crowd was astonished at His teaching.

When evening came, they would go out of the city.

Mark 11.15-19

Imagine that you're a peasant farmer from the hills of Galilee. This week – like the majority of your fellow countrymen and women – you're making pilgrimage to Jerusalem for the Passover festival. In a sling carried across your chest is precious cargo. Not an infant, but the finest lamb from your small flock. A lamb over which you rejoiced when it was born last spring, for it was a lamb without blemish. A lamb suitable for Passover. Which meant that you wouldn't have to endure the long lines in the Temple to purchase an animal. Nor – more importantly – endure the hardship that that purchase would mean for your family. Because the price of a lamb in Jerusalem at Passover is ten times that of what you can charge for one of your lambs in the market in Capernaum.

But as the dusty road turns and begins its long ascent to Jerusalem, your hand absent-mindedly reaches for the purse at your hip, jangling with coins as you walk. Because you know all too well that your lamb still has to pass scrutiny at the Temple. And it's not uncommon for a lamb that was unblemished in Galilee to mysteriously develop a blemish once it reaches Jerusalem.

And so, you offer a quick prayer to your God, the God of the exodus, which is the identity-defining story for your people, and the story you will tell once more at the festival. The story of the God who delivered your people from the tyranny of the pharaoh. The story at whose center lies the lamb now cradled to your chest. As your feet kick up dust on the steep road up to Jerusalem, you pray earnestly that when you arrive your lamb will be accepted...

Later that day you find yourself standing in one of those long lines in the Temple. You're in the outer court – the Court of the Gentiles – waiting to change the coins jangling on your hip at one of the tables arrayed around the walls. Because only Temple shekels are valid currency here, and you need to buy a lamb for Passover after all, because your lamb was rejected. Apparently not quite up to Temple, sorry, you mean, to *God's* standard.

You look across the court to watch other people buying their lambs. Or a couple of doves, the offering for the poor. Then your gaze lifts to take in the towering walls of the Temple. The extravagant wood carvings *are* quite beautiful, gold overlay still being applied here and there as Herod's great building project continues. As you near the front of the line and prepare to hand over the contents of your purse, a bitter laugh escapes your lips. Because the irony is not lost on you that in a few days' time your purchase will be offered to the God who once set people free from being forced to work on great building projects such as this.

Raised voices draw your gaze from the soaring walls back to the ground. People shift their feet to try and see the source of the commotion. And then, suddenly, the commotion is upon you, as one by one, the moneychangers' tables are upended, coins flying everywhere. You back away, and see a man striding across the courtyard to the booths where the animals are sold, where he proceeds to push the traders off their seats! Some grab their dove cages, but the man refuses to let them carry them off. And then you finally catch a glimpse of his face, and you see that rabbi, Jesus of Nazareth – the one that everybody is talking about – his eyes blazing fire.

You abandon the line to join the crowd gathering around him, to hear him say, "Is it not written, 'My house shall be called a house of prayer for all the nations'?" Then Jesus glares at a small knot of men dressed in fine robes, and declares, "But you have made it a robbers' den." You watch as the scribes hurry off, no doubt to report this outrage to the chief priests, and a chill of fear runs up your spine for this man who dares to interrupt the business of the Temple...

+ + +

Besides the accounts of the crucifixion and resurrection, a mere handful of stories from Jesus' life appear in all four gospels.

This is one of them.

John places it at the beginning of Jesus' public ministry in his Gospel, while we find it at the end of Jesus' ministry in the synoptic Gospels (Matthew, Mark & Luke). In Mark's Gospel, this story is the culmination of so much of what Jesus has said and done on his way to this moment. For this moment is the physical enactment of a parable Jesus told the scribes of the pharisees back in chapter three (verses 23-27). He had been accused by the scribes of being in league with the ruler of the demons, to which Jesus responded by telling a parable. He concluded by declaring, "No one can enter the strong man's house and plunder his goods unless he first binds the strong man." Often, we assume Jesus is referring to Satan as the 'strong man.' But Mark signals otherwise with his use of the word "goods," found just twice in his Gospel: in that earlier parable, and here, in this story, where Jesus refuses to allow the traders to carry their "goods" through the Temple.

That parable prepares us for what Jesus does in the Temple on this day. For Jesus has come to the Temple to challenge the structural injustice perpetuated by its ruling class, who control the mechanism of forgiveness, and thereby control the populace. As Mark's Gospel unfolds, Jesus has healed those declared 'unclean,' and forgiven those labeled 'sinner,' thus making it clear that he has come to replace the Temple as the center of healing and forgiveness.

The long-awaited Kingdom of God has finally come with Jesus, but it is not to be found where people assume it would be established, in the Temple. No, it is to be found among people at the margins, rather than among those at the center of power. The Kingdom has come to those who suffer at the hands of the chief priests and the elders, the Pharisees and their scribes, whom Jesus accused of laying heavy burdens on the people without being willing to lift so much as a little finger to help them.

It's no wonder that Jesus quotes from the prophet Jeremiah, saying, "You have made this House a robbers' den." Jeremiah delivered those words in the entrance to Solomon's Temple six centuries earlier, along with these words:

> "Thus says the God of Israel, 'Change your ways! Do not trust in deceptive words, saying, 'This is the temple of the Lord, the temple of the Lord, the temple of the Lord.' For only if you change your ways, truly practice justice between neighbors, if you do not oppress the migrant, the orphan or

the widow, then I will let you dwell in this place. But you are trusting in deceptive words to no avail as you steal and murder, swear falsely, commit idolatry and then dare come and stand before me in this house?" (Jeremiah 7.3-11)

Jeremiah tells his contemporaries that Solomon's Temple will fall. And now Jesus is saying the same will happen to this Temple, Herod's Temple. For the kingdom of God *has* come, but not to the powerful and wealthy, not to the bible scholars and purveyors of forgiveness. Instead, it has come to the poor, to the vulnerable, the excluded, to those exploited by institutional injustice. To people like this peasant farmer with his rejected lamb. Rejected by the very same people who have rejected Jesus. Those who have rejected the Lamb of God who takes away the sins of the world: the Temple officials, who will soon collude with the might of Empire to silence Jesus' outrageous challenge to 'business as usual.'

+ + +

As much as I may want to cheer Jesus on as he upends tables and sends 'those people' scrambling for their money, the view from the margins invites me to pause and ask difficult questions of myself. Because when it comes to matters of structural and institutional injustice, when it comes to questions of access and acceptance, the view from the place in society which I occupy is much like that of 'those people.' Remarkably privileged.

It just might be that both Jeremiah and Jesus offer a cautionary word to both our complacency and our complicity in systems and structures that continue to marginalize people. While we may like to imagine ourselves cheering Jesus on 2,000 years ago, this story causes me to consider whether I am – in fact – deeply invested in those tables staying exactly where they are.

Because 'business as usual' works pretty well for me.

+ + +

The Examen

1. Take a few moments to sit quietly and recognize God's presence with you.

2. As you think back over the reading, what are you most grateful for about what you read?

3. What feelings – comfortable and/or uncomfortable – arose as you read?

4. Choose one part of the story that particularly struck you and ask God what you're being invited to pay attention to.

5. Is there an invitation to take action of some kind? If so, make note of it, with the intention to follow through.

6. Rest in God's presence for a few moments.

Space for reflection – what did you hear?

SEAN GLADDING

Tuesday

And He looked up and saw the rich putting their gifts into the treasury. And He saw a poor widow putting in two small copper coins. And He said, "Truly I say to you, this poor widow put in more than all of them; for they all out of their surplus put into the offering; but she out of her poverty put in all that she had to live on."

Luke 21.1-4

My wife, Rebecca, often likens the bible to a landscape, and reminds me that my view of the landscape is determined by where I'm standing. Where we stand determines what we're able to see, and what we *understand* about what we see. We come to stand in the particular place from which we consider the landscape of the bible for all kinds of reasons: what we've learned from our families, from our church, from our culture, and for other reasons we're not even conscious of.

None of us have a complete view of the landscape, which is why it's so important to read scripture in communion with those unlike ourselves. But that, sadly, appears to be an increasingly uncommon practice. And so, when we open the pages of scripture to read, we put on the lenses which we've been given and through which we read. When we listen to scripture, we do so through the filters we have developed. When we hear stories such as this one, they've become so familiar that for many of us we can barely hear them anymore. We hear the beginning of the story and before we even reach the end, we already know what it's about.

My guess is that for many of us, as we began to read the story above, we started thinking about sacrificial giving, or giving "beyond the tithe" as I've sometimes heard. (Although, I suspect that most clergy would be delighted if the congregation just tithed!) Some of us might be thinking about building campaigns we've been part of, in which this story has featured in the preaching. Often, we imagine ourselves seated beside the disciples, looking on at this widow, and marveling at her generosity. But what is the view of this story from the margins, from the place this widow occupies in her world? What is *her* view of what's happening? Perhaps we might understand what's going on in this story differently if we could look through her eyes.

+ + +

Imagine with me for a moment that you're a woman living alone in the first century. Your husband died a few years ago, after falling from scaffolding on a building project here in Jerusalem. There was no other family to care for you, and so overnight you found yourself in desperate poverty. A friend of your husband took pity on you and offered you a corner of their one-room house in which to sleep. His wife found you work in the wealthy household where she is a cook. And so now, instead of sweeping the bare dirt floor of the house you once shared with your husband, you find yourself on your bony knees cleaning marble floors in the home of a Sadducee in Upper Jerusalem.

You're no stranger to hard work, but hours of cleaning every day have left your knees and back in constant pain, and your view of life has been reduced to a few square feet of marble, a long walk in darkness to and from this villa, and the little corner of the house where you sleep. It's hard not to feel bitter about your lot, but bitterness is a luxury you can't afford. So, instead you try to focus on your gratitude for having a roof over your head and food in your belly, and those few small coins that remain after you've given your hosts payment for room and board. The last two coins of which you clutch in your fist today, as you walk through the Temple. Because desperate poverty does not release you from your obligation to contribute to the Temple treasury.

As you approach the large, wooden chests in the treasury, you hang back, as there's a crowd of people making gifts today. After all, it's Passover, and the streets are crowded with pilgrims, many of whom are also making their annual offering to the Temple treasury. You watch as people in fine robes drop purses into the chests. More than one smiles as their coins make a satisfying jingle as they hit the pile below. You wait until the numbers thin out a bit, and then walk over as quickly as your old bones will allow. You look at the two coins in your hand for a moment – the last you have. And then you drop them into the chest. They make no sound as they hit the pile. You try and offer a prayer of thanksgiving for being able to contribute to the building of the House of God, but the words can't quite get past your lips.

You turn to leave and notice a group of men watching you. One is gesturing towards you. Embarrassed by this unwanted attention you quickly move away. As you leave the Temple grounds to return to work, you find yourself wondering who that man was, and what his interest in you could possibly be...

+ + +

Maybe the widow that Jesus pointed out that day *did* give her gift to the Temple with joy. Maybe she *did* offer a prayer of thanksgiving as she dropped those two tiny coins into the chest. Regardless, what Jesus points out is clear – however she gave it, she *did* give her all. Because the words that Luke uses to describe her gift literally mean, "her very life." So, *is* Jesus praising her generosity? *Is* this widow an example for us to emulate? Perhaps.

But, then again, perhaps not.

Immediately before this, Jesus is teaching his disciples with the crowds listening on, and he says this:

"Beware of the scribes, who like to walk around in long robes, and love respectful greetings in the marketplace, and chief seats in the synagogue, and places of honor at banquets... The scribes, who devour widow's houses, and for appearance's sake offer long prayers: these will receive greater condemnation."

"Beware those who devour widow's houses..."

And then Jesus looked up and saw *this* poor widow, and points her out to his disciples, as if to say, "See – there it is, happening right before our eyes." A poor widow, one of the people that God repeatedly says through the Law and the Prophets should be cared for by the community. For she is part of the most vulnerable population in ancient Israel – the orphan, the widow, and the migrant – those not under the care and protection of a landowning male.

Here is one more widow. Someone who it's – perhaps – not unreasonable to think ought to be able to come to the Temple (which is being built to the glory of the God who commanded Israel to care for women like her) and *receive* what she needs to live. But instead, she is expected to *give* what little she has left. Perhaps that's why, immediately after this, when some were pointing out the beauty of the Temple, Jesus says,

"As for all this, the days will come where there won't be one stone left upon another – it will all be torn down"

Because this House – the institution of the Temple – contributes to the systemic oppression of the very people it ought to serve. And every morning this week, crowds will gather early in the temple to hear Jesus condemn those who profit from the institution. Luke goes on to say,

"The chief priests and the scribes were seeking how they might put Jesus to death, for they were afraid of the people."

I'm sure they were.

The view from the margins offers a very different understanding of this story than the one I've heard most of my life. But, if I'm honest, I prefer the view of the story that portrays this poor widow as simply an example of generosity. Because all *that* view requires of me is to consider giving more generously from my excess.

The view from the margins is more disturbing.

Because *that* view highlights and confronts the structural injustice that both creates and sustains the disparity between the wealthy and the poor. A disparity which today is ever widening. A disparity which it is often easy to ignore because of the physical distance we tend to maintain between the over-resourced and the under-resourced.

Jesus pronounces judgment on the entire Temple system that fails in its duty to care for the most vulnerable of society. Were Jesus to walk the streets of the place where we live during this Holy Week, what might he point out to *us*?

+ + +

The Examen

1. Take a few moments to sit quietly and recognize God's presence with you.
2. As you think back over the reading, what are you most grateful for about what you read?
3. What feelings – comfortable and/or uncomfortable – arose as you read?
4. Choose one part of the story that particularly struck you and ask God what you're being invited to pay attention to.
5. Is there an invitation to take action of some kind? If so, make note of it, with the intention to follow through.
6. Rest in God's presence for a few moments.

Space for reflection – what did you hear?

Wednesday

Now when Jesus was in Bethany, at the home of Simon the leper, a woman came to Him with an alabaster vial of very costly perfume, and she poured it on His head as He reclined at the table. But the disciples were indignant when they saw this, and said, "Why this waste? For this perfume might have been sold for a high price and the money given to the poor." But Jesus, aware of this, said to them, "Why do you bother the woman? For she has done a good deed to Me. For you always have the poor with you; but you do not always have Me. For when she poured this perfume on My body, she did it to prepare Me for burial. Truly I say to you, wherever this gospel is preached in the whole world, what this woman has done will also be spoken of in memory of her."

Matthew 26.6-13

It's now just two days before Passover, and once more Jesus has left Jerusalem to spend the night in Bethany. Perhaps because the city has become too dangerous for him, and he still has that one last Passover meal to share with his disciples. Or perhaps, simply, because he wishes to spend time with friends who love him ahead of the horror that he knows awaits him.

A meal, a safe place to lay his weary head, and the warmth of companionship.

And in that place, a woman makes an extravagantly generous gesture of love. It's another one of the few stories to appear in all four Gospels. Matthew's account is almost identical to that of Mark's. John places his account a few days earlier, on the night before Jesus enters Jerusalem, where it takes place in the home of Mary and Martha. Mary is named as the one who anoints Jesus' feet with oil, while Judas is named as the disciple who complains about this waste of resources. Luke places the story earlier in Jesus' public ministry, in the home of Simon the Pharisee, where it is an unnamed woman who anoints Jesus' feet with oil. Although that woman bears the stigma of being known as a "sinner."

As we continue to consider the view from the margins, what do we see in this story? Or rather, *who* do we see? Our attention, after all, is so focused on the woman's actions, I wonder if it's easy to overlook the person whose home this is.

Simon the leper.

+ + +

Imagine that you're the host under whose roof Jesus is spending the night. The roof of a house that has been in your family for generations, but which for many years provided no shelter for you.

Because once the priests confirmed that the marks that had appeared on your skin were indeed leprosy, you were cast out of your village, forced to live with others like yourself.

Lepers.

Living in caves, or under canvas in the desert. Perpetually, ritually unclean. You are literally a walking socially communicable disease.

Leper.

That is all anyone needed to know about you. Your life reduced to a diagnosis, to a disease. Every social interaction with anyone who was not like you beginning with these words:

"Unclean. Keep away. Unclean."

It didn't take long for that word to malform your soul, even as the disease malformed your body. If there is anyone more marginalized than a leper, well, you don't know who they are.

But then came that day.

The day when you heard the rabbi from Galilee was in town. The one who healed people – even people like you. And so, mustering what little hope and faith remained in you, you risked provoking the anger of the crowds, dared rejection and violence. And – wonder of wonders – Jesus healed you! After the priests confirmed the witness of your now unmarked skin, you could finally return home.

But people still keep their distance.

You catch their sidelong glances in the marketplace. You notice that even family members can't help but check your hands while they're talking to you. And you know that you are no longer Simon, son of Judah. You are Simon, the leper – and always will be. A person of suspicion, someone who rarely shares table fellowship with anyone else. The disease may be cured – but the stigma remains.

But not tonight!

Tonight, your home is *filled* with people. For Jesus is in town for Passover, and he and his disciples are reclining at table with you. You listen to the disciples discuss all that Jesus has said and done in the Temple, excitement in their voices and writ large on their faces. But when you look at Jesus, you see other emotions etched into *his* features. His brow furrowed, his eyes... haunted. But as you watch, his eyes focus on something beyond the table, and his face relaxes.

Your gaze shifts to see what has caught his attention, and you observe a woman walk hesitantly behind your guests. When she reaches Jesus, she kneels behind him. Conversation quietens around the table as the others notice. And then suddenly the room is filled with the heady scent of nard, as the woman breaks a jar and pours the costly oil in a stream over Jesus' head. As the oil drips from Jesus' beard and hair, you hear one of the disciples complain to his neighbors about the waste. He goes on to suggest that a better use could be found for the money that perfume is worth. Others join in, loudly enough for the woman to hear, and she leans back, lowering her head, embarrassed. But Jesus interrupts the disciples to defend her actions.

"Leave her alone."

Earlier this evening you had heard the disciples discuss Jesus' talk of his death at the hands of the Temple officials, but it appears none of them believe it will actually come to that.

But this woman – apparently – does.

Because Jesus tells the disciples that she has prepared his body for burial. Then he says,

> "Truly, I say to you, wherever this gospel is preached in the whole world, what this woman has done shall be spoken of in memory of her."

While you ponder his words, you notice one of the twelve – Judas Iscariot – get up from the table and walk out into the darkness...

+ + +

Simon the leper.

That's really all we know about him. That he lives in Bethany, and that he was a leper. He must not have suffered from the disease anymore, otherwise he couldn't be living in the village. Nor share a meal with Jesus and the disciples. *Did* Jesus heal him? We don't know. But they obviously know each other well enough for Simon to host him. And even though Simon must know that Jesus is a marked man, he invites Jesus to break bread with him, thus declaring his allegiance to this man, assuming whatever risk that means.

But the relationship goes both ways.

For, in receiving the hospitality Simon offers, Jesus aligns himself with this marginalized individual, just as he has done with so many others throughout his public ministry. Jesus sees past the identifying, marginalizing label, "leper." He refuses to accept that Simon is someone to be avoided, someone to be viewed with suspicion. Instead, he sees Simon as someone to share a meal with. Someone to be embraced.

Who are the "Simons" in our lives?

What labels, what identifiers do you and I give people that marginalize them? Labels that communicate,

> "View this person with suspicion."
> "Keep your distance from them."
> "Don't be associated with them."

Labels that take no account of all that that person is. But, rather, labels that reduce them to a single word, so we can distance ourselves from them.

Labels that perpetuate the fear that divides us.
Labels that reinforce our own sense of superiority.
Labels that fuel the hate that leads to violence.

Who is "Simon the leper" for you and I? Who might Jesus be inviting us to look beyond the label to see the person? And – importantly – not just to invite them into *our* space, but to choose to join them in *theirs*?

In just a couple of days, Jesus will experience the horror of crucifixion. The ultimate marginalization.

I wonder if the scent of that perfume lingered in his hair and beard just enough that through the stench of sweat and blood and loosened bowels, with every tortured breath Jesus could inhale the aroma of love and friendship. The kind of love and friendship of which our world is in desperate need.

Love and friendship we will often miss out on if we only see certain people as "lepers."

+ + +

The Examen

1. Take a few moments to sit quietly and recognize God's presence with you.

2. As you think back over the reading, what are you most grateful for about what you read?

3. What feelings – comfortable and/or uncomfortable – arose as you read?

4. Choose one part of the story that particularly struck you and ask God what you're being invited to pay attention to.

5. Is there an invitation to take action of some kind? If so, make note of it, with the intention to follow through.

6. Rest in God's presence for a few moments.

Space for reflection – what did you hear?

SEAN GLADDING

Thursday

Now before the Feast of the Passover, Jesus knowing that His hour had come that He would depart out of this world to the Father, having loved His own who were in the world, He loved them to the end. During supper, the devil having already put into the heart of Judas Iscariot, the son of Simon, to betray Him, Jesus, knowing that the Father had given all things into His hands, and that He had come forth from God and was going back to God, got up from supper, and laid aside His garments; and taking a towel, He girded Himself.

Then He poured water into the basin, and began to wash the disciples' feet and to wipe them with the towel with which He was girded. So He came to Simon Peter. He said to Him, "Lord, do You wash my feet?" Jesus answered and said to him, "What I do you do not realize now, but you will understand hereafter." Peter said to Him, "Never shall You wash my feet!" Jesus answered him, "If I do not wash you, you have no part with Me." Simon Peter said to Him, "Lord, then wash not only my feet, but also my hands and my head." Jesus said to him, "He who has bathed needs only to wash his feet, but is completely clean; and you are clean, but not all of you." For He knew the one who was betraying Him; for this reason He said, "Not all of you are clean."

So when He had washed their feet, and taken His garments and reclined at the table again, He said to them, "Do you know what I have done to you? You call Me Teacher and Lord; and you are right, for so I am. If I then, the Lord and the Teacher, washed your feet, you also ought to wash one another's feet. For I gave you an example that you also should do as I did to you. Truly, truly, I say to you, a slave is not greater than his master, nor is one who is sent greater than the one who sent him. If you know these things, you are blessed if you do them.

John 13.1-17

Imagine with me, for a moment, that you are a servant in the household of a wealthy family, living in Upper Jerusalem during the first century. It's the evening before Passover. You expected to be working late into the night, making preparations for that most special of feast days tomorrow. But the house is hosting many guests *this* evening, who are gathered in the upper room, where they will share a meal together – without the household itself.

Unusual, for sure.

But you're just a servant, so you don't ask questions. Even though you are *most* curious as to why one of the sons of the household set off into the city earlier today carrying a water jar, and then returned a while later with these thirteen men. But you're young, still learning what is expected of you. So, you keep your head down for the most part, grateful that there is kindness in the household you serve, as you know that that's not always true for servants in other households. But, as the lowliest of servants in the household, you acknowledge that you're *not* grateful that washing the feet of guests as they arrive is your responsibility. But it *is* most necessary, if the guests are to enjoy the aromatic scents of the meal.

Rather than endure the aromatic scent of unwashed feet.

The mistress of the household instructed you to attend to the guests and take instruction from the rabbi as to what the needs of his small school of disciples were. So, when they arrive, you have the basin and towel prepared with a pitcher of fresh water from the well in the courtyard. But as the rabbi – Jesus of Nazareth – enters the room through the stairs from the courtyard, he tells you that your services will not be required this evening. You reach for the pitcher, so you can at least wash their feet before leaving. But Jesus lays his hand on your arm and says, "That won't be necessary tonight."

You look down at his feet, and think, *It looks necessary to me.*

Then your gaze returns to the face of the rabbi, this man who has caused such a stir in Jerusalem this week. Such a stir, in fact, that the main topic of gossip among the other servants all day has been why your mistress is hosting him tonight. For some of her neighbors are among those most offended by his actions – and his words. As your eyes meet, he simply smiles at you and indicates that you can leave. But your curiosity gets the better of you, and you linger at the top of the stairs, in the shadows, to see which of his disciples will do the task *you* would normally do.

But one by one they walk past the basin and towel and recline at the table.

You wait for their rabbi to instruct one of them to wash everyone's feet. But he doesn't, and they begin to eat the meal you laid out earlier. You know you should hasten down the stairs to join the others working in preparation for the Passover, but you find that you can't tear yourself away from your view here in the shadows.

After a while, Jesus rises from the table, lays aside his garments, and picks up the towel that is draped over the bowl. You watch, amazed, as *he* pours water into the basin and then begins to wash his disciples' feet! Some of whom look most embarrassed by this. *And rightly so!* you think. When he comes to one disciple, the man exclaims,

"Lord, will you wash *my* feet?!"

To which Jesus responds, "You don't realize what I'm doing now, but you will understand later." But the disciple refuses to let Jesus continue, saying, "You will *never* wash *my* feet!" Jesus replies,

"Unless I wash your feet, you have no share with me."

At which the man exclaims, "Then wash my hands too! Wash my head!" As Jesus cups water in a hand and pours it over the man's feet he says something else, but you decide you have lingered long enough, and don't catch it. As you walk down the stairs to your other duties, you wonder what the other servants will make of the story you have to tell of a rabbi taking your role – the lowliest servant in the household – to wash his disciples' feet.

+ + +

The tradition of the Roman Catholic Church is that this last supper Jesus shared with his disciples took place in the home of Mary, the mother of John Mark. Mary is briefly mentioned in the Book of Acts, where many are gathered in her house to pray for Peter who is in prison, Suddenly Peter is there, a servant girl so astonished, she leaves him standing at the gate.

I don't know if it was Mary's home where Jesus ate that last supper, but I like to believe it was.

Maybe Mary was one of the wealthy women in Jerusalem who financially supported Jesus' itinerant mission with his twelve disciples. Wealthy enough to host them for this special meal. Wealthy enough to have servants – servants who were not needed that night. Whenever I read this passage, one section always gives me pause. It has such a dramatic feel to me – the climax of a long, drawn out narrative: "Jesus, knowing that the Father had given all things into his hands, and that he had come from God, and was going to God..."

Did what?

If you were hearing those words for the first time, what would you expect to come next? Jesus making some grand, sweeping final declaration? Or revealing an apocalyptic secret to his disciples? Probably not the words that do follow:

> "...got up from the table, took off his outer robe, and tied a towel around his waist. Then he began to wash his disciples' feet..."

Jesus does what no one else has apparently thought to do. The most basic act of hospitality that normally a servant – or, occasionally the host – would perform, but which none of the disciples were apparently willing to do for the others. After Jesus finished, he said, "If I, your Lord and Teacher, have washed your feet, you also ought to wash each other's feet. For I have set you an example, that you also should do as I have done to you."

+ + +

When was the last time someone washed your feet?

Or that you washed someone else's feet?

52

It's not something most of us do on a regular basis. Maybe only *ever* for someone who – for whatever reason – cannot wash their own. Our family was part of a faith community that observed Holy Week in very intentional ways, including gathering on Maundy Thursday to wash each other's feet. It often felt awkward, uncomfortably intimate. Sometimes humorous, occasionally joyful. Always meaningful. But it was just once a year. Part of the liturgical rhythm of Holy Week, the view of that last week in Jerusalem we have gained from centuries of Christian tradition.

But what is the view from the margins?

What might we learn from the perspective of that servant? Who watched as Jesus humiliated himself before those who called him 'Lord,' causing Peter to rebuke his master. Because Jesus – once again – is enacting the great reversal of the Kingdom of God.

Where the first shall be last.
The greatest, the least.
The master, the servant.

It somehow all sounds so...right. Something we can aspire to. Something we can emulate. But we don't wash the feet of our guests anymore. So how *do* we embody the example Jesus set his disciples, which was much more than simply taking care of a practical need. Because Jesus was fully conscious of the enormity of what he was about to experience at the hands of the Temple and Roman authorities. Yet – knowing all that – he took off his robe, picked up a towel.

And washed his disciples' feet.

Humbling himself one last time before his ultimate humiliation: crucifixion on Jerusalem's landfill. For this story is about humility – about a right understanding of ourselves. It is about acknowledging our privilege, our power, our rights, our entitlement.

And then laying all that aside for the sake of others.

For greater love has no one than this – that a person lays down their life for their friends. As Jesus surely will just a few hours after washing his friends' feet.

I wonder how much time passed before the young servant lingering in the shadows that night found himself having his *own* feet washed, prior to joining his mistress to share a meal at that very same table. As a new community – the church – was formed. A community that would scandalize the Roman world, for upending the way society was so carefully structured.

Whose feet are you and I being invited to wash? What posture of humility can we adopt that would scandalize the carefully structured society in which we live?

+ + +

The Examen

1. Take a few moments to sit quietly and recognize God's presence with you.

2. As you think back over the reading, what are you most grateful for about what you read?

3. What feelings – comfortable and/or uncomfortable – arose as you read?

4. Choose one part of the story that particularly struck you and ask God what you're being invited to pay attention to.

5. Is there an invitation to take action of some kind? If so, make note of it, with the intention to follow through.

6. Rest in God's presence for a few moments.

Space for reflection – what did you hear?

SEAN GLADDING

Friday

Two others also, who were criminals, were being led away to be put to death with Him.

When they came to the place called The Skull, there they crucified Him and the criminals, one on the right and the other on the left. But Jesus was saying, "Father, forgive them; for they do not know what they are doing." And they cast lots, dividing up His garments among themselves. And the people stood by, looking on. And even the rulers were sneering at Him, saying, "He saved others; let Him save Himself if this is the Christ of God, His Chosen One." The soldiers also mocked Him, coming up to Him, offering Him sour wine, and saying, "If You are the King of the Jews, save Yourself!" Now there was also an inscription above Him, "THIS IS THE KING OF THE JEWS."

One of the criminals who were hanged there was hurling abuse at Him, saying, "Are You not the Christ? Save Yourself and us!" But the other answered, and rebuking him said, "Do you not even fear God, since you are under the same sentence of condemnation? And we indeed are suffering justly, for we are receiving what we deserve for our deeds; but this man has done nothing wrong." And he was saying, "Jesus, remember me when You come in Your kingdom!" And He said to him, "Truly I say to you, today you shall be with Me in Paradise."

It was now about the sixth hour, and darkness fell over the whole land until the ninth hour, because the sun was obscured; and the veil of the temple was torn in two. And Jesus, crying out with a loud voice, said, "Father, into Your hands I commit My spirit." Having said this, He breathed His last.

Luke 23.32-46

Today, we come to the seeming end of Jesus' journey this week, a journey which, for Jesus, began back in chapter 9 of Luke's Gospel, where Luke tells us that Jesus "set his face like flint to go to Jerusalem," knowing full well what would await him there. The view from the margins today may be the hardest for us to experience. But let us try.

+ + +

Imagine that you are a young man. An *angry* young man. A young man who rages against the occupation of your homeland, who despises these Roman pagans who pollute and defile the land of Israel. Pagans whose architecture and monuments and symbols of empire are beginning to dominate the landscape of your beloved country. And whose legions are garrisoned throughout the land to maintain the *Pax Romana*.

And, of course, to ensure you pay your taxes.

60

Your rage and zeal drove you into the wild hills of the North, where you banded together with others like yourself. Freedom fighters, ready to strike a blow against the enemy whenever you could. Living off the land as much as possible, but also accepting the support of family and friends and any others sympathetic to The Cause. Although you are ashamed to admit that when times were hard you were not above stealing livestock from your countrymen, even though you knew the hardship that would cause. But you were fighting *for them* – and one day they would understand.

You have burned tents set up for the collection of taxes on the main roads into Galilee. You have killed more than a few of the collaborators who robbed their own people. And a Roman soldier or two has felt the sting of your blade as they staggered drunk through the streets of the garrison towns.

But all that has come to an end now.

You had come to Jerusalem for Passover with your band of men, but not just to participate in the Festival. A carefully staged ambush of a squad of Roman soldiers had gone wrong, and you and one of your comrades had been captured. No swift death on the spot for you like the rest of your men. It is Passover, and the Romans intend to make a display of you, to remind a cowed populace of the severe penalty for challenging Rome's rule.

So, they march you through the narrow streets of Jerusalem, together with another man. Not a bandit like you and your friend, but that rabbi you heard speak in Galilee that one time. Jesus of Nazareth, who some believed to be the long-awaited Messiah: the promised King, the *true* Son of David. Not like those sycophantic pretenders, the Herodians. You spit reflexively. As you glance at Jesus' face, you see bruises like the ones that adorn your own, but you wince at the sight of the blood and sweat trickling down his face from the wreath of thorns jammed on his head.

Just a few days before, talk of Jesus had been all over Jerusalem. For he had come down from Galilee for the festival, and a huge crowd had formed around him on the road up from Bethany. Some had cut and begun waving palm branches – one of the symbols of your people that the Romans had outlawed. Everyone was praising God with joy, singing one of the psalms of ascent over and over again:

"Blessed is the King who comes in the name of the Lord!"

When you heard about that, for a moment you wondered, "Is *this* the time? Is *he* the one? Will God *finally* deliver us from our enemies, and restore the kingdom to Israel?" But now, as you glance over at the bloodied and battered man stumbling beside you, too weak to even carry the cross beam, you shake your head. Whatever dreams of freedom you might have dared to entertain have surely come to an end.

You finally reach the place they call 'The Skull,' and you see the poles waiting for the three of you. You thought you would be strong, but you find yourself beginning to shake uncontrollably, as you know all too well the kind of death you are about to face. Soldiers tie your arms to the cross beam and then lift you onto the pole, where you will slowly asphyxiate. After you've drawn your final, rasping breath, your corpse will be left to rot there, an example to others of the price of defying Caesar's rule.

You watch as those same soldiers now strip Jesus naked, as if crucifixion was not humiliating enough. They drive nails through his wrists into the cross beam and then lift him onto the pole between you and your friend. As the soldiers step back, their gruesome work complete, the crowd that has followed moves closer towards you. You are surprised to see a few members of the Sanhedrin here – easily recognizable by their luxuriant robes – and they start to jeer at Jesus. You look across and see those bloodied and cracked lips move in prayer as he looks down at the crowd and the soldiers. You strain to hear what he's saying.

> "Father, forgive them, for they don't know what they're doing."

You look down at the soldiers and think, *No, they know exactly what they're doing*. Your arms begin to ache, and your breath is now coming in shallow bursts. You look down as the rulers address the crowd, mocking Jesus: "He saved others; let him save himself, if *this* is the Christ of God, God's Chosen One!" And they laugh. But few others among the small crowd join their laughter.

As your pain intensifies, you find yourself turning towards the man on the cross beside you. You notice the inscription nailed on the post above his head, which reads, "This is the King of the Jews." *Who ordered them to put that up there?* you wonder. The soldiers now step forward again, adding their mocking voices to those of the rulers. Holding up a sponge dripping with sour wine, its vinegary scent assailing your nostrils, they say, "Yes – if you are the king of the Jews, save yourself!"

Then your friend adds his voice to the mockery, although you recognize his words come more from a place of despair: "Are you not the Christ? Save yourself...and *us*."

And suddenly something opens up inside you. In this darkest moment, a light begins to shine. You turn your body painfully towards your friend and say, "Do you not fear God, since you are under the same sentence of condemnation? But you and I – we deserve our fate." Then you turn back towards Jesus, and say, "But this man has done nothing wrong." Then you look below.

You see the mocking faces of the members of the Sanhedrin.

You see the soldiers rolling dice for his clothes.

You see the women weeping.

Then you turn back to Jesus, to find his gaze meeting yours, an expression you do not quite understand on his face. You look up, to read the inscription above his head once more. And then you turn back to those battered features, to those tear-filled eyes and say,

"Jesus, remember me when you come into your Kingdom."

Even as you hear yourself say it, it sounds so ridiculous. This man – and you – are going to die here.

And yet.

As you look at him, somehow you know you *have* found the longed-for Messiah. Not the one you expected, the one who would take back the kingdom by force at the point of a sword. But one who, instead, takes away the power of the sword – and empire – by allowing it to do its worst to him. You see him smile through the agony and hear these words,

"Truly I say to you, today you *shall* be with me in Paradise."

You hold his gaze for a moment, and then close your eyes slowly, the most unlikely of smiles playing at the corner of your mouth, as darkness suddenly begins to fall...

+ + +

That is the view from the margins on this Good and terrible Friday. And in some ways, we share the same view as that crucified bandit, even though we are separated by two millennia. For we, too, must look upon Jesus' broken body on the cross and decide for ourselves who and what we see there. Dare we believe, dare we hope that here lies the greatest reversal of all in the Kingdom of God? That all the power and might of empire – where death is the ultimate weapon of the tyrant – are rendered powerless by the One who takes that violence upon himself?

The One who does not offer violence in return.

All those who looked on from a place of power and privilege that day failed to see who it was they crucified. But those on the margins – even this dying bandit – could see the Truth. The Truth that would set them free. And so, they chose to embrace Jesus, following him into this very different kind of kingdom, the Kingdom of God that was – and *is* – coming on earth as it is in heaven.

+ + +

The Examen

1. Take a few moments to sit quietly and recognize God's presence with you.

2. As you think back over the reading, what are you most grateful for about what you read?

3. What feelings – comfortable and/or uncomfortable – arose as you read?

4. Choose one part of the story that particularly struck you and ask God what you're being invited to pay attention to.

5. Is there an invitation to take action of some kind? If so, make note of it, with the intention to follow through.

6. Rest in God's presence for a few moments.

Space for reflection – what did you hear?

Saturday

"Now the women who had come with him out of Galilee followed after, and saw the tomb and how his body was laid. And they returned and prepared spices and perfumes.
And on the sabbath day they rested according to the commandment."

Luke 23.55-56

Today is Holy, or Low Saturday, the day that lies between Jesus' death and resurrection. Guards have been posted outside Jesus' tomb; the women have mixed spices with which to embalm Jesus' corpse. All is quiet in Jerusalem, as it is the sabbath.

Unlike us, the women who prepared the spices do not yet know what they will find when they go to the tomb tomorrow morning. Today, all *they* know is that the customary peace of the sabbath has been ripped apart by their grief, for they have lost their friend, their rabbi, and the hope that this new way of living together had awakened in them.

Grief has a way of moving us to the margins. While life seemingly goes on as normal for everyone else around us, we may find ourselves withdrawing, pulling away to be alone with our grief, with our sadness and – sometimes – our despair. Because whenever we experience loss – whether the loss of a loved one, or a job, or a relationship, or our health – that loss is sometimes also accompanied by the loss of hope. Hope that we would live out our lives with our loved one. Hope that we would have financial security. That we would not be alone. That we would shoot hoops with our grandkids.

Hope that our tomorrows would be better than our todays.

+ + +

Imagine that you're one of those women, pouring and grinding the spices, mixing them, perhaps, with the tears that roll down your cheeks and drip from your chin. You grind the myrrh resin in the bowl, releasing its powerful aroma. You add aloe and some olive oil, and the embalming ointment begins to come together.

At first you work in silence, caught up in your grief, perhaps feeling intense pain, perhaps feeling numb. Jesus told you that it would come to this, and in some ways, you knew he was right. But that doesn't make this morning's task any easier.

The silence is broken by a stifled laugh, and you look up to see your friend cover her mouth, looking chagrinned. You stop your work, then wait expectantly. "I'm sorry," she says, "I was just remembering that time when Jesus..."

And so, you begin to tell your stories.

As you resume mixing the spices and oil, the tears continue to flow freely, but the tight bands of grief that squeezed your heart now ease a little, and there is more laughter as you share memories and stories. You remind each other of what Jesus taught you, and as you find his words on your lips, a warmth begins to spread through your chest. Jesus may be dead, but his teaching will live on in his disciples and his friends. You lift your chin in a determined manner. You will honor his memory by living out his instruction, in the community that formed around him.

Around *him*.

And just like that, the despair descends once more. Because Jesus is *dead*. Whatever will you do without him? This new way of living together, will it continue without him? Will you – a woman – still be considered just as much of a disciple as the men who followed him? The talk among the men last night was rooted in fear that the Temple authorities would come for his disciples next. Would the movement disband once you returned home from Jerusalem? Would it be a return to life as it had been before Jesus turned yours upside down?

The hope that Jesus awakened now seems so tenuous. As you finish mixing the spices, you realize that silence has once more fallen over the small group. You look around to find the same apparent concerns etched into the features of your companions. You wipe your hands on your apron, then lift it to your face as you begin to weep…

+ + +

Holy Saturday is the last day of the 'Bright Sadness' that is Lent. Some communities will spend the day reading the Gospels aloud together in anticipation of the joy that is to come tomorrow. Today is the day to dwell in the darkness of the tomb, to grieve Jesus' death, and in that place to acknowledge the darkness that we live with today. It is a day to name and grieve all the losses we suffer and endure. It is a day to lament the injustice that continues to be inflicted on the vulnerable, on the dispossessed, on those with little if any power, on all those who live at the margins.

For most of us, this will be just another Saturday. We will run the usual weekend errands, take kids to soccer games, maybe pull out the lawnmower for the first time this year. For a few of us, we'll be putting the finishing touches to our Easter morning sermon, trying to find something fresh to say about the old, old story. But before we do all that, let's take some time to sit with the women as they grieve their loss, and get in touch with all the losses we have endured, and lament the enormity of the losses of others.

To sit, for a moment or two, in the darkness of the tomb. In the profound darkness that comes just before the dawn…

+ + +

The Examen

1. Take a few moments to sit quietly and recognize God's presence with you.

2. As you think back over the reading, what are you most grateful for about what you read?

3. What feelings – comfortable and/or uncomfortable – arose as you read?

4. Choose one part of the story that particularly struck you and ask God what you're being invited to pay attention to.

5. Is there an invitation to take action of some kind? If so, make note of it, with the intention to follow through.

6. Rest in God's presence for a few moments.

Space for reflection – what did you hear?

Easter Sunday

Now on the first day of the week Mary Magdalene came early to the tomb, while it was still dark, and saw the stone already taken away from the tomb. So she ran and came to Simon Peter and to the other disciple whom Jesus loved, and said to them, "They have taken away the Lord out of the tomb, and we do not know where they have laid Him." So Peter and the other disciple went forth, and they were going to the tomb. The two were running together; and the other disciple ran ahead faster than Peter and came to the tomb first; and stooping and looking in, he saw the linen wrappings lying there; but he did not go in. And so Simon Peter also came, following him, and entered the tomb; and he saw the linen wrappings lying there, and the face-cloth which had been on His head, not lying with the linen wrappings, but rolled up in a place by itself. So the other disciple who had first come to the tomb then also entered, and he saw and believed. For as yet they did not understand the Scripture, that He must rise again from the dead. So the disciples went away again to their own homes.

But Mary was standing outside the tomb weeping; and so, as she wept, she stooped and looked into the tomb; and she saw two angels in white sitting, one at the head and one at the feet, where the body of Jesus had been lying. And they said to her, "Woman, why are you weeping?" She said to them, "Because they have taken away my Lord, and I do not know where they have laid

Him." When she had said this, she turned around and saw Jesus standing there, and did not know that it was Jesus. Jesus said to her, "Woman, why are you weeping? Whom are you seeking?" Supposing Him to be the gardener, she said to Him, "Sir, if you have carried Him away, tell me where you have laid Him, and I will take Him away." Jesus said to her, "Mary!" She turned and said to Him in Hebrew, "Rabboni!" (which means, Teacher). Jesus said to her, "Stop clinging to Me, for I have not yet ascended to the Father; but go to My brethren and say to them, 'I ascend to My Father and your Father, and My God and your God.'" Mary Magdalene came, announcing to the disciples, "I have seen the Lord," and that He had said these things to her.

John 20.1-18

Today we reach the conclusion of our sojourn in first century Jerusalem, where we have tried to imagine ourselves at the margins of society, from which place we have observed the events that unfolded around Jesus during the week of Passover.

For those of us who have participated in the life of the church for a long time, it's all too easy for the stories of what happened in Jerusalem that week to become routine in their familiarity – no longer able to surprise or shock or confuse us. And because the position from which we view them is so often profoundly privileged, we tend to imagine ourselves right next to Jesus, among the twelve disciples, looking on as an insider.

As someone who understands what's happening.

As someone with the benefit of 2,000 years of church history and of the many Easter services in which we've participated and in which we've re-lived these stories, year after year. That position of privilege has often made it hard to see things any differently than the way we always have. But this week we have tried to do just that, by considering the view from the margins, from the perspective of those with little – if any – access to places of power and privilege, both then and now.

We have tried to imagine what was it like to watch what Jesus did, and hear what Jesus said from the perspective of those who suffered marginalization under the dominant social narratives of his day. To seek out the vantage point of those who suffered under the systemic and structural injustices perpetuated by the institutions of power, not least the Temple itself. We have watched Jesus confront those institutions and people with immense privilege, most of whom were apparently unmoved by the plight of their fellow citizens. People who never questioned the institution, because the institution served them well. And – after all – did they not speak and act for God?

It's no wonder that those offended by his words and actions – those in the ruling class, who fear the people, because they hang on Jesus' every word – decided to conspire with the might of Empire to silence the threat that Jesus represented. It's no wonder that they bore false witness against him at the farce they called a 'trial.' It's no wonder that they manipulated the State to execute him, and then mocked him as he was dying: "some Savior you are."

Once they're satisfied that Jesus has paid the ultimate price for daring to challenge the way things are, they walk away, their work done, to enjoy the Passover feast. No doubt congratulating themselves for successfully maintaining their ritual purity throughout all the unpleasantness, so they can gather at the table with their families to tell the old, old story of the exodus. The story of the God who liberates people from oppression and slavery and tyranny.

While Jesus' battered and bloodied body will be lying cold in a borrowed tomb.

And while his closest friends hide in an upper room together, fearful that they will share Jesus' fate.

During Holy Week we have moved to the margins to get a view of Jesus confronting the Powers that maintain social systems that cause the misery and suffering of so many. Like the prophets of old, he has shone light on the darkness of Israel's leadership, and their response has been to attempt to squelch the light. Which is what institutions – and those who benefit from them – tend to do whenever their power is challenged or questioned. Both in the first century, and in the twenty first century.

Now, *we* know – as John tells us at the beginning of his Gospel – that the Light has come into the world, and that the darkness has *not* overcome it. But in the darkness of that *first* Easter morning, Jesus' friends were grieving his death, and everything must have seemed very dark indeed. So, imagine one more time that you are in Jerusalem for that Passover, almost two millennia ago...

+ + +

You're a heartbroken, fearful woman, making your way through the dark, narrow streets of Jerusalem before the sun rises. You carry spices and oil to anoint the body of your friend. One final act of love for this man who has changed your life.

How long had you lived with those voices in your head, voices that plagued you night and day? How many countless hours had you spent wandering the streets of Magdala in dialogue with beings no one else could see? People shunned you, threw insults – and the occasional rock – at you, fearful that they might end up like you. You, with your ragged clothing, unkempt hair, your arms bloodied and scarred from the constant clawing of your fingernails.

There are few more marginalized than those oppressed by the demonic.

But then came that oh, so wonderful 'before and after' moment – the day when you met Jesus, who liberated you from your

83

oppression, and restored you to sanity, to your family, and to your community. Jesus, whom you have loved and followed, a faithful disciple, determined to see others experience the same liberation he had given you. But now you are utterly bereft.

For Jesus is dead.

Humiliated. Brutalized. Dead. His body lying cold in a stone tomb.

You can still scarcely believe it, but you are determined to offer one final act of love to the man who set you free. So, you and a few of the other women make your way through the dark streets, walking in silence, tears blurring the outline of the cobblestones as you somehow manage to keep placing one foot in front of the other.

As you enter the grounds of the cemetery, you realize you will need help to roll away the stone that sealed the tomb in which Jesus' body has been laid. But as you walk through the garden and draw near, you see that the stone has already been rolled away. You hesitate, and then stride forward, going into the deeper darkness of the tomb. As your eyes begin to adjust to the darkness, you suddenly realize there is no body lying on the stone bier before you. The tomb is empty. Who has removed Jesus' body – and why?

You run back through those same streets to tell Peter and the others, who immediately take off running themselves. You follow after them, but you're exhausted, both physically and emotionally. You stumble back to the garden, alone. You walk up to the tomb, but you cannot enter. You stand outside, weeping. Then you gather yourself, and slowly walk into the tomb once more.

Through your tears and in the strengthening light of early morning you see two figures in white – but clearly not Peter and John. One stands at the foot, the other at the head of the place where Jesus had been laid.

"Woman – why are you weeping?"

You reply, your voice shaking, "Because they have taken away my Lord..." You glance down at the spices you're surprised to find you're still carrying, then continue, "and I do not know where they have laid him." You hear a sound outside. You turn around and walk out, to find a man standing outside the tomb, who asks you the same question as the others:

"Woman, why are you weeping? Who are you looking for?"

Supposing him to be the gardener, you say, "Sir, if you have carried him away, tell me where you have laid him, and I will take him away." You don't even stop to ask *how* you will carry his body, or where you will go. You just cannot stand the thought of him being abandoned here. Your eyes well with tears once more, and you begin to turn away.

"Mary."

You know that voice! You spin around...and there he is! Jesus! Alive! But, how...? "Rabbi!" you cry and throw yourself into his arms. Jesus says gently, "Don't cling to me, for I have not yet ascended to my Father. Go to my brothers and say to them, 'I ascend to my Father and to your Father, to my God and your God."

And then he is gone.

For a moment you just stand there, stunned. But then you find yourself running back through the streets once more, tears streaming down your face. But now they are tears of joy! You burst in on the disciples, startling them, and proclaim aloud,

"I have seen the Lord! And he told me to tell you this..."

+ + +

What does it mean that Jesus appeared to Mary first?

After all, Peter and John also ran to the tomb after Mary told them Jesus' body was missing – but they didn't see him. What does it mean that a once-demonized woman becomes the very first apostle – one sent to proclaim the message of the resurrection?

While the Temple rulers lay asleep in their beds, content after another successful Festival; while Pilate lay asleep in the Governor's palace, secure in the knowledge of Rome's power in this backwater of the Empire; the One they had tried to silence – for fear of the people over whom they exercised power – has been raised from the dead by the God whose story had once more been told at Passover. The God who is now bringing a *new* exodus: liberation from the oppressive power of sin and death. Death: the ultimate power of the tyrant.

Resurrection is *bad* news for those in power. But for those on the margins – on the thin and ragged edge of life – resurrection is *good* news. For all of us who suffer the oppressive power of sin and the fear of death, resurrection is *very* good news.

It is good news for the woman who prepared the spices yesterday, for now her question is answered: they will not have to try to continue this new way of living without Jesus, because Jesus is alive! The Temple authorities may breathe threats against those who follow Jesus, but what power do those threats have in light of resurrection? Jesus has moved those who live on the margins of society and Empire into the very center of what God is doing on earth as it is in heaven. For the Kingdom of God is indeed coming at the margins, and it is from there that we will catch the best view of Jesus, both in Jerusalem two thousand years ago, and wherever we may live today.

And so, the question before us at the culmination of our journey through Holy Week is this: how do we begin – or continue – to move towards the margins? To move from the spaces of power and privilege and abundance that we occupy, to spend time with the vulnerable and marginalized around us. To begin to forge the unlikely friendships that characterized Jesus' life. To hear Jesus' invitation to "Come, follow me" to the margins.

To accept the invitation to share a meal in the home of "Simon the leper," whoever that may be in our own context.

To listen to the voices of those who protest their plight and the injustices they suffer at the hands of those in power, rather than ignore or try to silence them because we don't approve of how they are protesting.

To discover who the "poor widows" are around us, and ensure that when their last coins are spent, they don't go without the basics of life, because friends don't let friends go without.

To offer a smile that says, "I see your humanity" to the person living with mental illness talking to themselves in the street, rather than giving them a wide berth.

To choose to stand on the other side of the serving line at our church's 'soup kitchen,' to take a plate and share a meal with those who so often come seeking more than just a plate of food.

Let's hear the invitation to seek and find beloved community at the margins, to forge unlikely friendships, and in doing so discover the presence of Jesus in our midst, who continues to bring the light and joy of Easter into the darkness with which we live.

As we walk out of Holy Week tomorrow morning, may we find ourselves determined to continue to catch a view from the margins.

+ + +

The Examen

1. Take a few moments to sit quietly and recognize God's presence with you.

2. As you think back over the reading, what are you most grateful for about what you read?

3. What feelings – comfortable and/or uncomfortable – arose as you read?

4. Choose one part of the story that particularly struck you and ask God what you're being invited to pay attention to.

5. Is there an invitation to take action of some kind? If so, make note of it, with the intention to follow through.

6. Rest in God's presence for a few moments.

Space for reflection – what did you hear?

About the Author

Sean Gladding is a storyteller with a particular passion for introducing (or reintroducing) people to the Story found in the Bible, and to confront some of the harmful ways this beautiful, challenging, messy story is sometimes told.

He is the author of *Ten: Words of Life for an Addicted, Compulsive, Divided and Worn-Out Culture,* and *The Story of God, the Story of Us* (one of Relevant Magazine's top ten books of 2010).

Originally from Norwich, England, he makes his home in the MLK neighborhood of Lexington, Kentucky. There he and his family grow food with others, raise chickens, kick a soccer ball when it's dry and play board games when it's wet.

Visit www.seangladding.com

A final note from the author:

I am grateful for the encouragement of those who support my writing through the Patreon platform, and whose partnership helps get projects like this one out into the world:

Audrey Booher
Bruce Nicol Jr
Clay Everitt
Ericka Engen-Graham
Katy Shultz
Marcie Timmerman
Matt Russell
Peter Johns
Steve Pavey
Tracy Norton

To learn more about becoming a Patron, visit my page:

https://www.patreon.com/seangladding

Made in the USA
Middletown, DE
12 March 2020